Life LIGHT
THE WORKBOOK

DOING THE WORK TO STAY LIT

AYANA THOMAS

For permission requests and more information, write to the author at foryoulibertywrites@gmail.com.

Liberty Writes
Washington, DC
Printed in the United States of America

ISBN: 978-0-578-61043-6

Liberty Writes

NOTE TO READERS

Welcome to Life Light: The Workbook!

You are here because you recognize the need to move forward in your journey. I applaud you for taking this step into deeper purpose and greater awakening. *Life Light: The Workbook*, is here to guide you. Listen to yourself – your experiences, your wisdom, your intuition. You have the power within yourself to be boundless and to reach your own personal greatness.
Be patient with yourself and celebrate your wins along the way. You are important and your contributions are necessary in this world!

Stay on purpose, stay free!

Ayana

Lighting The Way Forward

Life Light: The Workbook contains direct quotes from *Life Light* to help guide your deeper reflections. The light bulb indicates that a quote from the book follows. The light bulb also helps you to differentiate the Life Light quotes from the workbook commentary. Finally, the light bulb also serves as a point of reference, in case you want to go back to the book to read the quote in context with the rest of the chapter.

Reflection

Life Light: The Workbook does not include reflection prompts. However, you can practice the **Liberty Writes 24-Second Rule™** anytime you need to take a break, reset, or reframe your thoughts. Close your eyes and take three deep breaths. This should take you about 24-seconds to complete. These deep breaths help to center you and give you a break from the racing thoughts in your mind.

Please honor the need for reflection and stillness in your life. Recognize the need to put the book(s) down and be present with yourself. It is important for you to focus your thoughts and listen to your inner voice. Some thoughts might be intimidating initially. Do not let that deter you. When you have made the necessary discoveries and come to the necessary conclusions, take some notes and continue working!

BOOK 1 *Knowing*

- Consistently Lit
- Journey/Evolution
- Mindwholeness
- Knowledge and Learning
- Perspective
- Trauma

REFLECTIONS:

- Your Role in Vision
- Stay in the Now
- Manifest
- On Words...

BOOK 2 *Being*

- Connectedness
- Love
- Children

REFLECTIONS:

- Identity
- Reputation
- O.Y.S.
- Ask for Help

BOOK 3 *Becoming*

- Freedom
- Peace
- Grace
- Purpose

REFLECTIONS:

- Stewardship
- Know Your Worth
- The Power of Choice
- Cultivating
- Clarity
- Abiding In Difference

BONUS *Section*

- Liberty Writes Word Bank
- Revolutionary Reads
- Thomas Model of Individual Learning
- Thomas Model on Teacher/Student Duality
- AAHR Model for Navigating Trauma
- Present and Accounted For
- Clarity Cleanse
- Works Cited/Referenced
- Meet the Author & Liberty Writes

BOOK 1
Knowing

Consistently Lit

Open Life Light to the Consistently Lit chapter.

Keeping The Light On

There was something about having the light on that made me feel safe enough to put my trust in sleep; to believe that I would be safe throughout the night and more importantly that I would wake up again when the sun took its position in the sky the next morning.

Did you sleep with a night light at any point in your life? Why did you sleep with a night light? How did it make you feel? Do you see the benefit of keeping the light on in a physical and metaphorical sense?

Vision Casting

I purpose time on New Year's Eve to sit quietly, listen for direction, and develop my goals for the year ahead. Not long ago, the direction that I received was "to be a light in the world".

In *Life Light*, I described my vision casting process for each New Year. How do you plan your goals for each New Year? What are your 1 year, 5 year, and 10 year goals?

Being Able to See With Boundless Vision

Light enhances the ability to see; see what is immediately in front of you, behind you, and around you. More importantly, light gives you the ability to see beyond you, as far as vision will take you. Our humanity will only allow us to go as far as we can see, before fear sets in and our pace slows (sometimes to a screeching halt). There will be times when you will have to proceed into some darkness to reach purpose. Your ability to maintain clear vision will have a profound impact on your long-term success.

My dad told me that I could have anything that I want as long as I was willing to do the work. My interpretation of what he said is that my life is boundless. I can go as far as I want and accomplish as much as I want to accomplish – as long as I do the work. What are you doing to create unnecessary boundaries or limitations in your life? What plans do you have in place to help you pursue the boundless possibilities in your life?

Keeping the Light On

Keeping the light on is more than a figure of speech - action is consistently required for you to keep the light on.

What conditions (relational, environmental, etc.) make you feel safe, protected, and courageous? What steps do you need to take to keep your light on?

Being Light for Others

We have to be in tune with the needs of others - those in our close circle and those we do not even know. You never know how acknowledging someone, a total stranger, can help them to feel seen, relevant, and necessary in this world.

We have the power to be light for someone else - to reassure them that things will get better or to encourage them to walk boldly through some life circumstance that is challenging them. Just by being present - you can help someone to feel safe, protected, and cared for. Also, your presence as light, can help others to see.

Who are you lighting the way for? How often are you present (physically, mentally, emotionally, etc.) to model light for others?

CONSISTENTLY LIT

Chapter Tri-Fecta!

What were your takeaways from the chapter?

What was most impactful?

Where do you need to do some additional work?

Journey/Evolution

"Don't worry about what to do with your life,
create the life you want."
- Unknown

Open Life Light to the Journey/Evolution chapter.

There is so much direction and meaning in this quote - such a vibe. The quote suggests that it is more important to focus your energy on actively working towards the life you want, than it is to be stuck focusing on perfecting the master plan for your life.

How do you define success for your life? How close are you to reaching your definition of success? Are you open to the reality that what you want might change over time?

"Life is a journey - the path beyond the horizon, unseen."

I love this quote too!!! If you can't tell by now,
I love words.

**When you think about the path beyond the horizon...
unseen...what feelings do you get? Are you nervous,
terrified, overjoyed, excited, and eager? It is so important
to realize that the path beyond the horizon continues with
every step that you take forward. You cannot lose faith or
give up now. You have to keep pushing on.**

From my perspective (and pen), **to evolve is to follow the free flow of development over time, as you learn from and interact with yourself, your tribe, and the world around you.** The key, in my interpretation of the definition of evolve, is to follow. So many times we trick ourselves by thinking that we are in control. Having the discipline to follow is mastering (self) control.

In general, how comfortable are you following? Even as a leader, it is important for you to develop a comfortability with following. Are you a control freak? Do things have to go your way all of the time? How do you cope/manage when life does not go according to your plan(s)?

Evolution is trying to push you forward into something greater!

Are you starving your purpose to death trying to cling onto a reality that is not yours?

We have to stop reinforcing the behaviors and philosophies that teach us that there is only one way, the "right" way to do a thing. It is important though, that you are at least aware enough to know when a shift in the path is approaching so that you can adjust accordingly.

Write a List – Were you taught that there was only one way to do something? Make a list of those things below. Based on your review of the list, did you learn that any of these things could be done differently?

Letting go of the need to control someone else's life is very liberating for you and for that person.

Whose life are you in a position to influence? Are there areas where you are trying to control that person and their next steps? What can you do to empower the individual to take ownership of his or her life?

When you are honest with yourself and others, you are open to evolve. Evolution is required for completing the journey of life. Purpose leech thinking is flawed and detrimental to you reaching and living in your full potential.

Do you have purpose leeches in your life? How do you create boundaries between you and them?

Many times, those of us with influence try to stay out front too long and end up derailing the path for those that are coming behind us. Worse, we project our fears, failures, or other insecurities onto those we are trying to help.

Have you been in a situation where someone tried to project their reality onto you? Were you in the role of the mentor or the mentee? How did you work through this moment?

JOURNEY/EVOLUTION

Chapter Tri-Fecta!

What were your takeaways from the chapter?

What was most impactful?

Where do you need to do some additional work?

Mindwholeness

Open Life Light to the Mindwholeness chapter.

Mindfulness, in the simplicity of its original definition means thought. The western adaptation of the word has furthered the definition to include: on purposeful and present thought. Life Light enhanced the definition of the word mindfulness to include: present awareness of self, others, and the around (that is anything and everything around you).

Mindwholeness is the idea that the mind must be whole in order for you to have a proper relationship with yourself, others and the around.

Disorientation

Disorientation is actually a great tool in learning. We usually associate disorientation with someone who is confused, out of sorts, or lost. However, disorientation happens every time you encounter information or an experience that your mind cannot make meaning of. Disorientation forces you to evaluate what you see, hear, feel, and know. Welcoming disorientation and developing awareness around it so that when it happens you respond by reflecting, rather than avoiding these feelings is very important.

Usually when I encounter disorientation, I pause for reflection. I ask myself, "What do you feel and see? What are you thinking"? While disorientation is mostly triggered by our interaction with something outside of ourselves, how we recover and respond to disorientation is based on our internal construct – from mind to soul.

When was the last time you were disoriented? Did you embrace the moment to learn from it? Or did you disregard the feelings of disorientation and go back to business as usual? If you chose to learn from the disorientation, what process did you follow to get to the root of the disorientation?

Triggers

If you haven't read the Trauma chapter, you should. Our experience with trauma significantly affects our human function. In order to achieve mindwholeness, you have got to be aware of your triggers. Triggers can be associated with anything that reminds you of a traumatic memory.

Do you know what your triggers are? If so, list them here.

What do you do to limit interaction with your triggers?

If you cannot prevent interaction with your triggers, what do you do to protect yourself from suffering when triggered?

How You Cope

Knowing how you cope is necessary for mindwholeness. When you are aware of your coping patterns, you can more quickly assess any problems or situations to find the root of the problem and rectify the issue. That only happens when you are mindwhole.

What coping behaviors you do employ to reduce or avoid a stressful situation?

Stress Responses and Retention in the Body

When you can feel stress in your body, this level of intrapersonal connection between the mind and the body is called proprioceptive awareness. We all respond to stress differently.

Where do you carry stress in your body? Can you feel the shift in your body and energy when you encounter a disorienting situation or a trigger? What signals does your body send you? How do you respond when your body is alerting you that you are in a stressful situation?

MINDWHOLENESS

Chapter Tri-Fecta!

What were your takeaways from the chapter?

What was most impactful?

Where do you need to do some additional work?

Knowledge and Learning

Open Life Light to the Knowledge and Learning chapter.

I am so grateful that my lack of knowledge/information did not kill me or delay my purpose.

Knowledge is not static – it is evolutionary. Realizing this and reflecting on my life, there were so many times when additional information or knowledge could have been beneficial to me. I could have made wiser decisions. I could have avoided some heartache.

What are you currently doing in your life to pursue knowledge? Are there areas of your life where you wish you had some additional information or guidance?

Knowledge is static for some people because their knowledge has not been tested by a diversity of experiences or because they refuse to learn more.

It always amazes me when the news features someone that has grown up on a rural farm and had very little exposure to things outside of that environment. Even with the internet and the accessibility of information on cell phones, there are still people that do not pursue knowledge. Information comes at you all day, every day, but pursuing information for the sake of learning is an intentional behavior.

Have you encountered people that refuse to learn new information? How was your interaction with that person/ group of people? Was it difficult for you to engage with them? What did you learn from your observations of them?

When you do not know or cannot comprehend something, you become immediately defensive and resistant to whatever is around to protect yourself. Your ability to receive new information is limited and your behavior can become erratic. Feeling like you have adequate knowledge and more importantly knowing how to apply that knowledge is a necessary security for the human construct.

Friends – in these moments where new information makes you uncomfortable, be present with that feeling. Be willing to be vulnerable with yourself. It is ok if you do not know everything. Knowing everything is not even possible – so give yourself grace in that space. Do not be afraid to ask questions or spend time researching information until you get to the answer. That is how we learn.

Parents, teachers, role models and influencers have a responsibility to teach with a disclaimer: "This is what I know now. It presents as rock solid truth, but you may have a life experience that will present a different truth and that is ok. Go with what you know and grow as you go".

Would you have been better prepared to navigate the fluctuations in life if someone influential in your life would have taught you that knowledge is evolutionary? As an influencer, how will you present the knowledge that you have to share differently?

KNOWLEDGE AND LEARNING

Chapter Tri-Fecta!

What were your takeaways from the chapter?

What was most impactful?

Where do you need to do some additional work?

Perspective

Open Life Light to the Perspective chapter.

Perspective is your point of view, your attitude, or your way of regarding something. Your perspective really drives how you interact with the world, people in the world, and the circumstances that you encounter every day in the world.

Four Dimensions of Information Processing:

- Perspective – point of view, attitude, way of regarding something

- Bias – judgement made from information gathered in perspective

- Opinion – articulation of perspective

- Fact – information that can be proven by historical evidence or validated by calculation

It is important that you know what dimension of information you are operating in, when you are making decisions or drawing conclusions. My desire is that you check bias and opinion – through clear and objective perspective.

I envision perspective as a verb: subconscious action happening in real time. Perspective applies itself as a layer, a lens if you will, when past experiences collide with a present reality. There is an outward action associated with the mental patterns that are happening in the background to drive behaviors triggered by perspective.

Can you trace back any of your behaviors to a layer of perspective that you once had, that you later found out was not completely accurate? In other words, your perspective was wrong.

Regular checks to your perspective are necessary. Stepping back to evaluate situations before making decisions or reacting is critical.

We want to aim for clear, evaluated, tried and true perspective. Keep your eyes on reaching your destination. If the wind blows, dig your feet in and prepare to fortify your position. Anything else that pops up unexpectedly - acknowledge it, do what you can, but put these things in their proper place of perspective and treat them accordingly.

As a literal thinker, I usually try to skip past all of the fat and get straight to the meat. Maintaining a level of objectivity is super important in how you receive, perceive, and then act on information.

Identify three areas in your life where you need to be more objective. Use the chart below to evaluate your progress towards being more objective.

Areas for Objectivity	What do you perceive to be the issue with your perspective in this area now?	What will you do to be more objective?	Check in 30 and 90 days out.

PERSPECTIVE

Chapter Tri-Fecta!

What were your takeaways from the chapter?

What was most impactful?

Where do you need to do some additional work?

Trauma

Open Life Light to the Trauma chapter.

Trauma is the imprint left on a person (physical, emotional, psychological, or spiritual) as a result of an intensely stressful experience, moment, or circumstance. Trauma causes a tear in the fabric of your life and if it is left unaddressed, the fabric will continue to tear until it is no longer useful.

During one of my mirror dates, I noticed a scar.

What story does your scar tell? Can you share the story with others to process or work through a trauma they may have experienced?

An approach to remedy trauma includes acknowledging the trauma, addressing the trauma, healing from the trauma, and then reflecting briefly on the trauma (AAHR). For the sake of making a thing, a thing, let's call this the AAHR (pronounced air) Method for Navigating Trauma:

These are just a few examples of the many different ways to get at the problem. The important thing is that you actually take action. We can only pursue powered living when we are actually directing the actions to move us forward.

REMINDER: This is your life. Do what you need to do to heal - your way and in your perfect time.

MENTAL HEALTH RESOURCES
(Please reach out if you need some help!):

- Call 911 if you require immediate attention

- www.mentalhealth.gov or call 1-877-726-4727

- http://finder.psychiatry.org

- https://www.zocdoc.com

LIBERTY WRITES AAHR METHOD FOR NAVIGATING TRAUMA

Acknowledge	Address	Heal	Reflect
Awake to the reality that trauma is real and could be impacting the way you handle yourself and others.	Therapy Therapy Homework Journal Draw Dance Serve Others Action is required to address the presence of trauma in your life.	Consistent, deliberate energy directed towards the action of healing. Heal in your own time, your own way.	Reflect to see clearly the ways you have evolved. Clebrate those wins through reflection. Be honest about the areas where work still needs to be done.

TRAUMA

Chapter Tri-Fecta!

What were your takeaways from the chapter?

What was most impactful?

Where do you need to do some additional work?

BOOK 1

Reflections

Your Role in Vision

It is important to know your role in bringing vision to life. Visionaries see the end result. Most visionaries are extremely passionate and enthusiastic. This is a level of energy that every idea and every project needs to get mobilized. Visionaries see something magical that moves people to action. Many times though, visionaries are unable to carry out their vision alone, because their role is to see - not necessarily to do.

There are other contributors to vision who are incredible at hearing the vision and bringing it to fruition. Let's call these folks the executors (not executioners!!!). Executors are designed to get it done, by any means necessary. Executors are gifted to hear and see at the same time – which is an ability that is often overlooked. Executors have the tough task of carrying the weight of vision to completion and they often receive none of the glory for a job well done.

It is so important that you know if you are a visionary or an executor. That way, you do not waste energy trying to walk a path not designed for you. Additionally, it is important for you to know which one you are, so that you can surround yourself with the right types of people. If you are a visionary, you need a circle of executors. Otherwise, you and your visionary friends will be stuck with a multiplicity of ideas that you cannot bring to fruition. Similarly, if you are an executor, you need to be sure there are visionaries in your circle that can help you see when you're stuck in the details. We have to learn how to work in tandem to get ish done.

Stay In The Now

The present (what is happening now - in this moment) should get the majority of your attention. The past cannot be changed and the future cannot be controlled.

Only look back to the past, as an archeologist or an analyst for clues to inform your present and future, but leave the fossils behind. Leave the future to the greatest power and you will get to where you are supposed to be at the appointed time. Trust this truth and stay present.

Manifest

What you manifest is literally what shows up - everywhere you are. Sometimes you have to manifest an alternate (positive) reality, until you reach that place. That is why regular self-affirmation is so important. Sometimes you have to speak peace into chaos until you reach your place of peace. Or you may have to speak prosperity into a moment of limited resources. You are what you manifest. Manifest greatness!

On Words...

Words are so extremely powerful. They are the vehicles that we use to move thoughts and feelings. I am a 100% geek and I have an affinity for words. Don't judge me – my truth.

The power behind your words can break a person down or bring about their healing - literal life or death. All the words matter. That should be a hashtag...#allwordsmatter! The words you choose to wear on something as simple as a t-shirt sends a message to others or the message associates you with a group/organization before you even say anything. The words you plaster on the back of your car bumper sends a message to drivers behind you. The words you choose to hang up on posters and pictures on the walls of your home or office communicate messages to you - over and over again.

Pay attention to the words you use. Are you creating environments for you (and others) to thrive? Or are you being defeated by the messages you are taking in regularly? I choose to live and have chosen to use my words to help other people pursue powered living.

Say more with less!

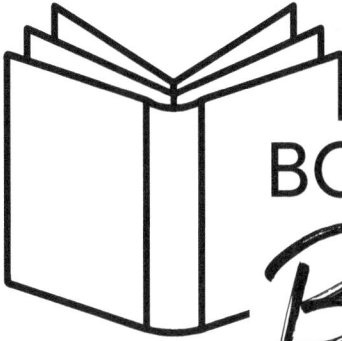

BOOK 2

Being

Connectedness

Open Life Light to the Connectedness chapter.

Many of the lessons we learn and many of the successes we have in life can be directly attributed to the connections we have to other people.

Make a list of the people you are connected to, who have significantly affected your life. Make time to thank them!

It is how you cultivate all of your connections that really matters.

Remember, cultivating is digging in and doing the dirty work to bring something to fruition or to develop something from infancy.

Let's start with your connections that need some work. Make a list of those connections.

Write a plan of action for ways that you can develop your connections. Check the list of revolutionary reads in the back of the workbook for resources that can help guide your action plan writing.

There are definitely benefits to being alone from time to time, but creating situations of complete isolation is detrimental to your wellness. You should be finding ways to grow and thrive in every evolution of your life. Having people around to agitate you enough to grow and sprinkle enough goodness on you to help you thrive makes all of the difference.

Who are the agitators in your life? Who are the people that pull out the best in you? Thank those people for their contributions to your life.

Necessity for Connection to Others

I have developed a greater intensity for making every moment count. Be intentional about connecting.

Think about the one or two (or more) people that you must talk to each day in order to feel a sense of contentment. How do these connections enhance your life?

Responsibility in Connection

More than doing the work, we need to be on the same page for the purpose of the connection - is this an acquaintanceship, a friendship, or are we in deep connection (familial or romantic).

LEVELS OF CONNECTION

Acquaintanceship

- association through some commonality – organization membership, familial association, community partnerships, etc.

- occasionally connecting in person/by phone/or social media or in passing

Friendship
(within friendship there are varying levels of closeness)

- mutually beneficial and equitable engagement

- stronger likelihood for vulnerability

- endures through each individual's personal evolution

- safe space for each individual to share energy and walk in their truth

Deep Connection

- friendship +

- familial connections are bound by blood, but require the same level of investment of long-term connections like marriage

- partnership agreements with mutual goals and shared support

- new life is the outcome deep connection – literally and metaphorically (offspring or the birthing of collective vision)

Based on this criteria (and some factors that you may want to include), how would you classify the people in your life? Objectivity and equity in connection is important. Make sure that you are honest and that you place people in the appropriate category – do not just squeeze people in where you would like them to be.

Evolution of Connection

As we evolve as individuals, it is necessary that our connections evolve as well. I think we struggle here a lot. If connections are not psychologically, emotionally, or physically safe, go your separate ways.

Based on your connection classifications, were you able to identify any connections where you need to create boundaries or sever the connection to protect your psychological safety? Were you able to identify any connections that require additional attention on your part?

Communicate to others that things are changing for you - even if you do not know how things are changing. The importance of communication (even in uncertainty) cannot be stressed enough.

Why is it so difficult to communicate when you recognize that you are evolving? Who do you need to update on your evolutionary status? How can you improve your communication with your connections, going forward?

CONNECTEDNESS

Chapter Tri-Fecta!

What were your takeaways from the chapter?

What was most impactful?

Where do you need to do some additional work?

Love

Open Life Light to the Love chapter.

Love is so deep and so diverse.

Think about your experiences with love – broad, vast, and deep. How would you define love? How do you want to see love expressed in your life (what you give and what you receive)?

When we begin to question love, what we are actually doing is questioning someone's commitment to you, his or her trustworthiness, and/or his or her ability to prioritize you.

If you have doubt or hesitation regarding love in your life, take some time for intentional reflection and observation. Write down your thoughts so that you can trace your thought path. What is the root of your questions? Can you safely address these questions with you loved one(s)?

As a child, watching love on display, it didn't seem full of joy.

How did you experience love as a child? How have you emulated what you experienced in your connections with others since then?

If you love someone, tell them. Our days are too short for you to overthink and not share your truth.

Who do you need to share your love with? Maybe you need to sow into a child or mentee more intentionally. Perhaps you need to reconnect to a long lost loved one. Perhaps you need to renew the zeal in your marriage. Open your mouth and tell someone that you love them. Yell it from the mountaintops. Do not let this opportunity pass you up. Hearing that you are loved – never gets old! However, you know that already!

LOVE

Chapter Tri-Fecta!

What were your takeaways from the chapter?

What was most impactful?

Where do you need to do some additional work?

Children

Open Life Light to the Children chapter.

We all have a responsibility to raise someone up, to walk in your footsteps. Raising children (yours or someone else's), is quite possibly the most important human responsibility ever (besides continuously raising yourself).

Who are you raising up?

Do you have kids? What warning labels did you need as you were/are raising your kids?

Want kids? What are you nervous about? What resources and tools do you have to support you through the child-rearing process?

Similarly, having kids is like having a mirror dangle in front of you reflecting your behaviors (good, bad, or indifferent) all of the time

The mirror reality was a tough pill for me to swallow. Recognizing that my child is watching my every move has certainly caused me to be intentional about what I display in front of my magical curtain.

Using the chart below, capture your current "mirror" behaviors and where you have opportunities for improvement. Make the time to think about this with intention. There are subtle things that your children/mentees may see that could have long-term impacts on their development, if not corrected now.

	Good	Bad	Unclear
Current Behaviors			
Areas for Improvement			

CHILDREN

Chapter Tri-Fecta!

What were your takeaways from the chapter?

What was most impactful?

Where do you need to do some additional work?

BOOK 2
Reflections

Identity

Just like knowledge and many other concepts covered in this book, identity is evolutionary. Have you run into someone that you have not seen in a while and they have said to you, "Wow, you've changed"? Yes, you may have changed. That's ok - especially if the change was intentional.

We are not created to be one dimensional beings. There are so many layers to who we are as individuals. Get to know who you are - at home by yourself, 1-1 with someone, in a group setting, etc. It is important for you to be comfortable in your own skin. There are so many layers to our identity - traversing layers is ok - we were not created to be one-dimensional.

Reputation

I had an epiphany not long ago that you cannot control how and when people speak on your character. I guess I have never really cared much about people's opinion about me. Even in failure - I know that I am great (my daddy told me so). So I had never really given any thought about the conversations people have about me when I am not in the room, until someone slipped up and mentioned that they had "just been talking about me".

This made me reflect on the number of conversations that could possibly be happening about me that I am not and may never be aware of. That was an instant gut check. My gut said "Listen kid…make sure you live your life in a way that people only have positive things to say about you". It is your choice what mark you leave on this earth. Only leave people with great things to say about you. You never know when and where your name will come up.

Own Your Shit (O.Y.S.)

Every now and then, you have to "talk to the people the way they need to be talked to"! It is so important for you to own your shit. You will make mistakes, but be quick to admit your fault. Forgive yourself and forgive others. Ask for forgiveness - even if you cannot identify anything that you've done wrong. Forgiveness is an act of purification that humbles you in the process. Walk in the weight of the responsibility of your truth. (SAY THAT OUT LOUD ONE TIME FOR THE PEOPLE IN THE BACK).

Walk in the weight (pause)

Of the responsibility (pause)

Of your truth (pause)

Do not create space for regret. Man up and live your best life.

PS. My mother and my mentors are probably rolling their eyes at me right now - but I made it through the whole book and only cussed once - well twice. Sometimes you have to "give it to the people the way they need it". Jesus will forgive me! That said, don't leave this moment and forget to OYS!

Ask For Help

I listen to and learn from everybody in my life. I really do. Not long ago, I had the opportunity to spend the weekend with my three-year-old Goddaughter. She is so smart and intuitive. At three, she is at the point in childhood development where she is extremely articulate – not necessarily with a filter of appropriateness. She says what she means and means what she says.

I went to help the G-baby get out of the car and she pulled away from me and said "I don't need help, I'm a big girl". Her reaction struck me in such a profound way. We spend all of our formative years rushing to grow up so that we can be Big Girls and Big Boys, who don't need help anymore. When we are young, we think we are invincible – able to do everything on our own. In reality, we receive help from someone, somewhere every day. More importantly, we should never be at a point in life when we are afraid or unwilling to ask for help.

No matter how wise, wealthy, or successful we are, there will always be someone that can come along to enhance our human experience. When they arrive on the scene – don't be too proud to ask for help!

BOOK 3
Becoming

Freedom

Open Life Light to the Freedom chapter.

Think back to the example of the angelic being in the Freedom chapter.

What does freedom look like to you? Write or draw your example. Remember there is blank space in the create space of the workbook.

Freedom is a mindset - a determination to refuse to allow the weight of the world to weigh you down.

Are you free within the space you currently occupy? Or are you self-obstructing?

I think formality puts restrictions on creative ingenuity and innovation. When my eyes were opened, I started stumbling upon simple things that I didn't realize could be so freeing. What I appreciate about freedom is that the more liberated you are, the more liberated you can become.

Take a moment and think about the simple things in your life that create so much internal conflict. Are there things that if you changed them today, your disposition as a person would change? You have to make a decision to pursue peace and to follow freedom at any cost.

More importantly, this caused me to be thoughtful about the ways my perspectives and approach towards life may have caused others to not feel free around me. I only want to project good vibes into the atmosphere. I never want to make anyone feel like they cannot show up authentically. You have the ability to give grace and to empower others to live their truth aloud.

How can you empower others to live in their truth? Practice this behavior in the next week.

FREEDOM

Chapter Tri-Fecta!

What were your takeaways from the chapter?

What was most impactful?

Where do you need to do some additional work?

Peace

Open Life Light to the Peace chapter.

Peace is settling into an intrapersonal space of contentment, stillness, and overall unbotheredness. Peace is achieved in the absence of war – with yourself, others, and the around. War is a strong term to use here, but I want you to think critically about the ways in which you wage war (a literal battle) against yourself, others, and the environments around you, on a regular basis.

Pause for a moment and think about the things that prevent you from living in a state of peace. Take some notes to help you reflect now and in the future. What can you change immediately to increase your peace?

Everyone and every situation is not receptive to the power of peace.

Have you been in a situation that was not receptive to the power of peace? How did you resolve the situation? What have you learned from reading the Peace chapter that can help you make peace with someone's unwillingness to walk in peace?

I had to address the peace blockers and create (sometimes uncomfortable) boundaries to protect my peace. In an effort to protect your peace, you may have to create a list of guiding principles to help people understand how to interact with you. Having this list of guiding principles makes your expectations very clear to you and the people you interact with on a regular basis.

For example, your list of guiding principles may look a little like this:

Here at Ayana's Safe Space Inc., we are committed to thriving in peace by:

- Staying objective

- Regularly reviving our energy

- Avoiding toxicity

- Immediately stopping anything that kills our vibe

- Choosing the peaceful path

- Speaking to each other with love and truth

Use the space below to write 3-5 Guiding Principles for Your Peace. You are creating boundaries to protect your peace. What behaviors from others will help you to reach this state of peace?

We have the responsibility to manifest and cultivate peace constantly. Peace is a state of being. Be Peace.

PEACE

Chapter Tri-Fecta!

What were your takeaways from the chapter?

What was most impactful?

Where do you need to do some additional work?

Grace

Open Life Light to the Grace Chapter.

In many ways, grace is the real MVP. Grace has an impeccable track record of successes – namely keeping us on the appropriate path to reach our destiny. We don't give grace enough credit as the silent partner that makes a major investment in our lives. Thank you grace!

We all have been empowered to stand in the gap and extend grace to others. We have the power to give someone something they don't deserve. Similarly, we have the power to prevent someone from receiving a punishment/consequence that they should receive. Use this super power wisely.

What are the ways that someone has given you grace? How can you extend grace to others?

Move to Action: Over the next week, be intentional about giving grace to someone in your life. How does this make you feel? What have you learned about receiving grace, through your experience giving grace to others?

Giving grace goes along with giving people the freedom to evolve. When you extend grace, you are giving someone permission to make mistakes and feel their way through life in a safe space that allows them the opportunity to learn along the journey.

How do you see grace aiding someone's evolutionary journey?

GRACE

Chapter Tri-Fecta!

What were your takeaways from the chapter?

What was most impactful?

Where do you need to do some additional work?

Purpose

Open Life Light to the Purpose Chapter.

Purpose is more about what you were created to do to make an imprint that enhances the world. That's heavy, but you may never read anything else I write. So I am putting the pressure on now! What you were created to do is big! Treat it that way.

How acquainted with your purpose are you?

___ I do not know my purpose.

___ I do not know where to start.

___ I know my purpose, but I procrastinate or avoid purpose altogether

___ I am taking steps towards walking in my purpose.

___ I am working to incorporate purpose into my work/life balance

___ I live in my purpose full time.

___ I find purpose in my work.

What are you most passionate about? What gives you the greatest sense of joy and peace? When are you most fulfilled? What are you most troubled by when you see it happening?

Are you doing the work that aligns with the responses to these questions?

Continue to surround yourself with the elements of purpose and eventually, the light will come on. You will be in the right place, at the right time, to step into your own greatness. I promise.

Use the space below to capture notes about your purpose progress based on the stage of purpose you identify with most.

Life Light Stages of Purpose

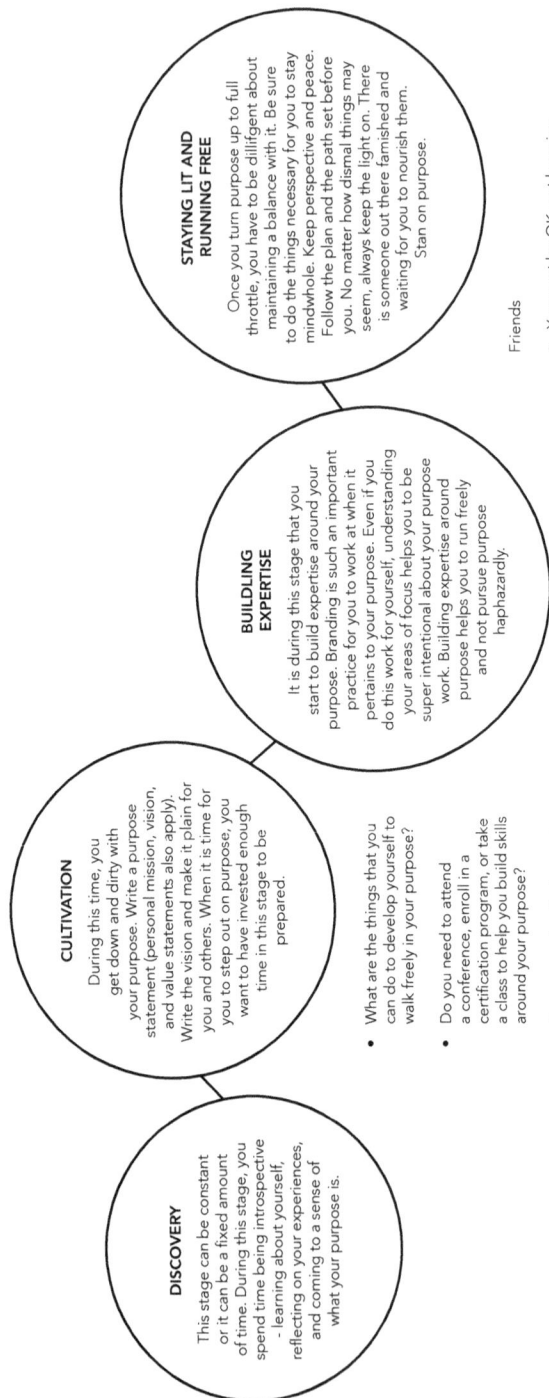

DISCOVERY

This stage can be constant or it can be a fixed amount of time. During this stage, you spend time being introspective - learning about yourself, reflecting on your experiences, and coming to a sense of what your purpose is.

CULTIVATION

During this time, you get down and dirty with your purpose. Write a purpose statement (personal mission, vision, and value statements also apply). Write the vision and make it plain for you and others. When it is time for you to step out on purpose, you want to have invested enough time in this stage to be prepared.

- What are the things that you can do to develop yourself to walk freely in your purpose?

- Do you need to attend a conference, enroll in a certification program, or take a class to help you build skills around your purpose?

- Do you need to find a mentor or a therapist that can help you work through this stage of forming your purpose?

BUILDING EXPERTISE

It is during this stage that you start to build expertise around your purpose. Branding is such an important practice for you to work at when it pertains to your purpose. Even if you do this work for yourself, understanding your areas of focus helps you to be super intentional about your purpose work. Building expertise around purpose helps you to run freely and not pursue purpose haphazardly.

STAYING LIT AND RUNNING FREE

Once you turn purpose up to full throttle, you have to be diligent about maintaining a balance with it. Be sure to do the things necessary for you to stay mindwhole. Keep perspective and peace. Follow the plan and the path set before you. No matter how dismal things may seem, always keep the light on. There is someone out there famished and waiting for you to nourish them. Stan on purpose.

Friends

- You must be OK, not knowing what is next.

- Trust the Divine Order for your life! Stay in the flow of purpose and ride the wave.

- Pursue every new opportunity with intentionality and remain thankful for every blessing.

PURPOSE

Chapter Tri-Fecta!

What were your takeaways from the chapter?

What was most impactful?

Where do you need to do some additional work?

BOOK 3
Reflections

Know Your Worth

Shout out to Hip-Hop for gassing us up as a people to see the potential in ourselves, but more importantly, to know our value and what we bring to the table. So boom...I had a personal goal that got derailed because...life happens. Fast forward a few years and I was asked to help someone else do some work that would help them to reach their personal goal, which also happened to be the goal that I had abandoned. As I was helping this other person reach their goal -
a thought came to my mind "think about all of the ways that someone else has benefitted from your brilliance...monetize that." That hit me like a ton of bricks. Here I am just giving away my brilliance and all my purpose driven goodness for someone who probably knows my value, but is exploiting the fact that I do not know (or at the very least charge) my own value. Crazy, right?

So I sat down and calculated my per hour rate. Now of course, your per hour rate based on what you make at your job, may not be nearly what you perceive your worth per hour to be, but at least now you know your base rate. When someone asks you to do something (in business or as a favor), think about the energy and effort you will have to invest to deliver what they are asking you for. Don't just stop there. Calculate the cost for you to deliver. If there is no return on your investment, think carefully about whether or not this is something that you want to do. I started doing this before responding to requests and it significantly changed my way of thinking. Now I understand what it costs me to do something for someone else - in time, money, resources, and energy. This is so important. Set your price and don't be afraid to walk away when someone is unwilling to pay your worth.

A few inspirational personal value quotes, for your reading pleasure:

- "Raise the price, raise it two times"
  – Quavo

- "My success can't be quantified"
  – Beyoncé

- "Know yourself, know your worth"
  – Drake

- "I think I'm getting too much money, everybody mad."
  – O.T. Genasis

- "You hear that? That's the sound of the price going up"
  – Jay-Z

- "I invested in myself that means I'm black owned."
  – Lil' Baby

- "You measure time differently, when you know your cost per hour."
  – Ayana Thomas

- "You say no differently, but respectfully, when you know your cost per hour."
  – Ayana Thomas

- "You invest your energy differently, when you know your cost per hour."
  – Ayana Thomas

Stewardship

Are you a good steward? Not long ago, I was preparing to teach a class on the relationship between purpose and connectedness (Connectedness, p. 55). During my research process, I looked up the definition of stewardship and it blew my mind. I had mostly heard of stewardship in religious settings, associated with financial giving. Yes, giving is necessary in so many different contexts. However, the definition of stewardship includes so much more than merely giving. A steward is someone who helps to carry or bring forth something for someone – similar to a surrogate. Are you prepared to support someone else as they work to reach their full potential?

I am naturally a giver. Most of the time, I give too much. I offer too much. I say too much. I have had to learn boundaries so that I do not dry up my well trying to water someone else's garden. Maintaining boundaries is a very hard chore for true givers. As a giver and good steward, I have learned to give (of my time, of my experience, of my resources) in abundance, so that I can reap in abundance (in peace, in joy, in prosperity, in protection).

When you have the opportunity to be a steward for others, do so, genuinely. Do your part to help someone reach higher and go the distance. We want to see everyone win! Give a little. It won't kill you!

The Power of Choice

Having the ability to choose is such a powerful thing. Making choices is a brain behavior that we often take for granted. Similar to memory making, our brain makes choices constantly throughout the day that we are not always aware of. Do I walk the stairs or take the elevator? Do I pour my beverage in a cup or do I drink from a straw? Do I speak my mind or do I keep my mouth shut? These are all choices that we make. Don't get me wrong, there are far more complicated choices that we make on a daily basis. I used these examples to illustrate the frequency at which we make decisions that we give little attention to - they just come naturally. I have two points that I want to make on choice (and now that I am thinking out loud, this probably should have been a whole chapter - maybe a special feature for *Life Light: Part Deux*).

Back to my two thoughts - here goes:

Use the wisdom that you have to make the best choices that you can. As you grow in wisdom, you will make better choices. Do not beat yourself up for poor choices that you have made now or in your past. At the same time, don't get stuck on stupid or wallow in self-pity. Learn from the choices you've made, count the costs/weigh all of the options in future decisions and keep pressing on.

My second thought is this - many times folks get decision paralysis because there is fear associated with the risk of the choices you have to make. Rather than getting stuck in fear, see yourself in power or empowered to make a choice. As a strong, smart, and successful person (manifest these ideas even if you are not quite there), you have the power to make a choice that can enhance your now and next. What will you choose?

Clarity

Oh to be clear – to be seen clearly, to be heard clearly, and to see clearly. Clarity has two primary definitions: 1) to be coherent and intelligible and 2) to be transparent. When I think about clarity, I think about how uncomfortable it can be driving through a patch of fog. When you cannot see where you are going, your body has so many different reactions. As soon as the fog breaks, all of the anxiety and angst eases. Wouldn't it be nice if all of our days were totally clear?

Unfortunately, the way life works, we know that there will be cloudy days and days where the fog is so thick, that we don't feel like we can move forward. Some of us may even get stuck in this place for more than a few days, because we cannot function in the absence of clarity. I hope that **Life Light** has helped you develop a greater sense of clarity on the various topics included in the book. I hope that if you don't have clarity that you will do the work necessary to gain clarity – so that you can be fully present with yourself, others and the around. I also hope that you are able to use the strategies provided in this book to clear out the things in your life that may prevent you being able to see your purpose in a transparent way – no fog.

Every year, I complete a clarity cleanse to help me prepare for the year to come. It is a seven day cleanse that forces me to withdraw myself from life's unnecessary distractions (namely social media and Netflix binge watching), so that I can seek direction. Sometimes the circumstances of life will not allow you to physically separate yourself from home or work to get the direction that you need in life. The clarity cleanse is designed to help you tap into your divine source to obtain guidance that helps you reach towards your greatness. The clarity cleanse helps you to focus on reflection - asking yourself the tough questions and dealing with the tough realities. More importantly, the clarity cleanse will help you come to solutions that will help you to walk clearly towards your future.

I hope that you are clear on my intentions for you to reach your highest potential. More importantly, it is my hope that you succeed there. Be open to evolution and follow peace with every step.

Details for the Liberty Writes Clarity Cleanse are included in the bonus section.

Abiding in Difference

Of all of the words in the English language, abide is in my top 5. Abide is an action word that means dwell or live within. Oh, that meaning is so amazing! Other definitions of abide also infer two separate entities coming to agreement. Now that I have established the groundwork for abide – let me get to the point.

When I think of the word abide, I think about laying in a flower's leaves and the leaves closing over me. When you abide, you are enveloped. Whatever you are abiding in surrounds and insulates you. You can be abiding in metaphoric leaves, a blanket, a connection, a decision, etc. When I make the decision to abide with someone or something, I have a settling feeling in that moment. I find peace there. Abiding is a long-term behavior that requires your intentionality and your presence.

Each of us have unique qualities. Your intricacies and quirkiness is what makes you, you. There are times when something about you may not be in alignment with someone or something else. Just because there is difference in your midst does not mean that you pursue a path of conflict. It is important that you learn how to abide in difference – with yourself and with others. Learn how to sit there for a while – settle into grooves that were not created for you, but are intended to aid your personal development. Still yourself and find patience and tolerance for someone or something else.

Some of life's greatest lessons are discovered abiding in difference. In difference, you have an opportunity to explore areas that are potentially unfamiliar or uncomfortable. I have found great comfort in abiding in difference with others and learning to appreciate their qualities as opposed to judging or creating boundaries because of difference.

In an aggravating kind of way, I actually like to hear people unpack their unique qualities and experiences. I recognized that engaging difference allowed me to grow. We also tap into the power of abiding together in difference, when we linger long enough to exchange dialogue and determine what is blocking us from peace.

It is possible to abide and not agree! I like the concept of abiding together in difference better than agreeing to disagree. There is discord in disagreement. However, there is love and care in abiding together. I can genuinely support you in shared space, but not walk in the same footsteps. Abide in wisdom – Abide for the win!

Cultivating

I love the concept of cultivating. I use this word a lot in the business world to sound smart. Cultivating implies digging in (with your hands) and raising something from seed to fruit. A little different from manifesting, cultivating is the dirty work required to bring things (ideas, vision, etc.) to reality. There are times when manifesting is not enough. You will have to lean in and get some sweat on your brow. You may have to get a little dirt under your fingernails to reach your end goal. Don't stop now. Dig in and do the dirty work. Your future self will be very grateful that you did!

WELCOME TO
Liberty Writes
Create Space FOR
JOURNALING AND PURPOSE PLANNING!

When I read, I take notes everywhere – page margins, front/ back cover, any blank space I can find in the book. I am a BIG note taker! The repetition in taking notes reinforces learning application. I want you to walk away from your experience with Life Light having learned a great deal – especially about yourself and the amazing things in store for you.

When I was designing *Life Light* and *Life Light: The Workbook*, it was important that there was enough space for note taking. This create space is here to provide you with additional space to pursue and plan for the next steps of purpose in your life. The create space can be used to affirm yourself in this present moment. You can use this space to begin your healing process in trauma discovery. The ways in which you can use this space are boundless. Flip the switch on your creativity!

When I am creating, I prefer a blank canvas. Sometimes trying to write neatly in the lines stifles creativity, triggering my OCD. So I wanted to be sure to include some lined writing space + some blank space for freestyling your thought flow. I hope you enjoy this create space. Make it your own!

_____

_____

_____

_____

_____

_____

_____

_____

_____

_____

_____

_____

_____

_____

_____

_____

_____

_____

_____

_____

_____

_____

_____

_____

_____

_____

_____

_____

_____

_____

_____

_____

_____

_____

_____

_____

_____

_____

_____

BONUS
Section

LIBERTY WRITES WORD BANK:

I enhanced or created new definitions for the terms included in the Word Bank.

Evolve – follow the free flow of development over time, as you learn from and interact with yourself, your tribe, and the world around you.

Freedom – making a conscious decision to live untangled from self-imposed or socially imposed expectations that confine your greatness

Trauma – the imprint left on a person (physical, emotional, psychological, or spiritual) as a result of an intensely stressful experience, moment, or circumstance.

Liberty Writes 24-Second Rule™ – anytime you need to take a break, reset, or reframe your thoughts. Close your eyes and take three deep breaths.

Mindfulness – present awareness of self, others, and the around (that is anything and everything around you)

Mindwholeness – the idea that the mind must be whole in order for you to have a proper relationship with yourself, others and the around

Peace – settling into an intrapersonal space of contentment, stillness, and overall unbotheredness

Perspective – happens when your past experiences collide with your present reality

READS THAT HAVE REVOLUTIONIZED MY LIFE:

1. *The Coldest Winter Ever* by Sister Souljah

2. *Single, Married, Separated, and Life After Divorce* by Miles Monroe

3. *Grace: More Than We Deserve, Greater Than We Imagine* by Max Lucado

4. *The Purpose Driven Life* by Rick Warren

5. *The Role of Meaning and Emotion in Learning* by Pat Wolfe

6. *Experience, Consciousness, and Learning: Implications for Instruction* by Barry Sheckley and Sandy Bell

7. *A Moment of Silence: Midnight III* by Sister Souljah

8. *Year of Yes: How to Dance It Out, Stand in the Sun, and Be Your Own Person* by Shonda Rhimes

9. *Battlefield of the Mind: Winning the Battle in Your Mind* by Joyce Meyer

10. *The Five Love Languages: How to Express Heartfelt Commitment to Your Mate* by Gary Chapman

11. *Me and My Big Mouth: Your Answer is Right Under Your Nose* by Joyce Meyer

12. *Blink* by Malcolm Gladwell

13. *A Second Chance: Grace for the Broken* by Keith Battle

14. *The Five Love Languages of Children* by Gary Chapman and D. Ross Campbell

15. *Me, Myself, and I Am* by Matthew Peters

16. *The Hard Questions: 100 Essential Questions to Ask Before You Say "I Do"* by Susan Piver

17. *Biblical Mathematics: Keys to Scripture Numerics* by Ed. F. Vallowe

What are the books that have revolutionized your life?
(Hopefully, *Life Light* is on your list – no peer pressure though)

_____

_____

_____

_____

_____

_____

_____

_____

_____

_____

_____

_____

_____

_____

_____

_____

_____

_____

_____

_____

_____

THOMAS MODEL OF INDIVIDUAL LEARNING

The Thomas Model of Individual Learning provides a systematic structure for measuring the effectiveness of information/knowledge transfer between teacher and student. This process of learning can be observed in simple tasks like learning how to tie a pair of shoes to learning complex STEM systems. Ultimately, teachers should aspire to have their students develop into teachers. In a traditional classroom, raising up students to be teachers enhances the peer-to-peer synergy and can increase the rate of learning.

MASTERY

TEACHING

When a student is able to successfully guide another student through this model, they have reached the mastery level of learning, which is teaching. Teachers are able to articulate the same information they were taught at base level, with an easiness and ability to adapt the information for various learning styles. Teachers are able to mesh complex concepts and return them to students in a comprehensible manner. Teachers remember their process of learning and desire to bring out the best in their students. They will be patient and draw from their learning experience to design an optimal learning environment for their students.

SUCCESSFUL APPLICATION

Reaching this level of learning is to be celebrated! After a period of repetition with the information, a student is able to successfully apply what they have learned without intervention from the teacher and without error. It was important to include this level of learning because so many learners try to advance from application to teaching without successfully applying what they have learned, over time. It is crucial that students invest the time at this level of learning, to master the intricacies of the information they are toiling with, so that they can function liberally at the highest level of learning.

APPLICATION

The goal of teaching should be to help students develop independence with the information you are sharing. At the application level, students have the ability to manipulate the information without the guidance of the teacher. In application, the student works through continued practice with the information. At this level, mistakes are made and the student is able to regroup and develop through trial and error..

UNDERSTANDING

Aha!...is usually what teachers hear at this level of learning. Students have developed to the level of understanding, when they are able to grasp the detail of the information that you have shared with them. For processes, students can at least, articulate the outcome or the goal of the learning exercise. In other fact based information sharing, students may be able to start piecing related concepts together.

PERCEIVING

Perceiving is the base level of learning. At this level, students come into contact with new information.Depending on the setting and the context, students may have the opportunity to interact with the information by problem solving or logic building. Learning for many people ceases at the perceiving level. This may be the case because students do not have the capacity to make meaning of the new information. This can also happen when the reinforcement necessary to advance to the higher levels of learning is absent.

INFORMATION TRANSFER

THOMAS MODEL ON TEACHER/STUDENT DUALITY

The Thomas Model on Teacher/Student Duality focuses on the interrelationship between the role of the teacher and the student. Equal action must be taken in order for synergy to be cultivated between the teacher and the student.

The model also demonstrates how an individual can traverse the boundaries between teacher and student. There are times when a teacher must be available to receive and process information as a student. Likewise, there are times when a student takes on the role of an instructor in a teaching moment.

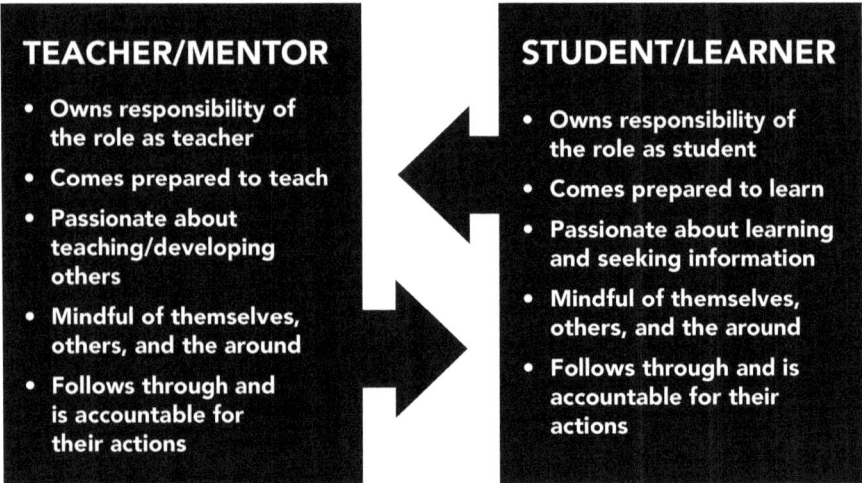

TEACHER/MENTOR

- Owns responsibility of the role as teacher
- Comes prepared to teach
- Passionate about teaching/developing others
- Mindful of themselves, others, and the around
- Follows through and is accountable for their actions

STUDENT/LEARNER

- Owns responsibility of the role as student
- Comes prepared to learn
- Passionate about learning and seeking information
- Mindful of themselves, others, and the around
- Follows through and is accountable for their actions

Teachers should exhibit these behaviors when they are preparing to SHARE information with their students (Teacher/Student):

- Become a student of the material first to learn as much as you can - this can include conducting additional research and pulling in additional resources to support the learning moment.

- Identify key lessons to share with your students.

- Consistently listen to your presentation as a student, when you are preparing to teach and as you deliver the content.

Teachers usually exhibit these behaviors when they have the opportunity to LEARN (Student/Teacher):

- Teachers should remove their teacher hat and become a sponge to the material being presented.

- Teachers can be critical of other teachers who are not prepared for the teaching moment.

- Teachers are consistently thinking of ways that they would teach the lesson.

LIBERTY WRITES AAHR METHOD FOR NAVIGATING TRAUMA

Acknowledge	Address	Heal	Reflect
Awake to the reality that trauma is real and could be impacting the way you handle yourself and others.	Therapy Therapy Homework Journal Draw Dance Serve Others Action is required to address the presence of trauma in your life.	Consistent, deliberate energy directed towards the action of healing. Heal in your own time, your own way.	Reflect to see clearly the ways you have evolved. Clebrate those wins through reflection. Be honest about the areas where work still needs to be done.

119

PRESENT AND ACCOUNTED FOR

Liberty Writes Exercise for Priority Planning and Mindwholeness

Make the choice now to be fully present!

Use this chart to organize/prioritize your thoughts and clear your mind so that you can focus.

STEP 1

Take two minutes and write down everything on your mind - nothing is off limits. Use the back of this page if you need more space.

STEP 2

From Step 1, what can you resolve on your own quickly now or in the immediate future? Write those things here.

STEP 3

From Step 1, what items require planning (LT or ST), partnership or delegation?
Write those things here.

Use this blank space to capture anything else that does not fit neatly into the boxes.
Now take three deep breaths.

LIBERTY WRITES CLARITY CLEANSE

Welcome to the Clarity Cleanse! I am super excited (like running, jumping, skipping, dancing, excited) that you recognize the need to go deeper and further into what is now and next for you! The next 7 days of your life will be pivotal. Please be sure you read through and understand all of the instructions before you begin the cleanse. Please be sure to take notes and plan time for the cleanse daily.

To complete the cleanse, you will need to do the following:

1. **Identify Your Why**
    What do you need clarity about? Why aren't you clear? Take some notes to help you reflect out loud.

2. **Identify 3 Focus Areas**
    Narrow your notes down to three focus areas. For example, I have focused on (1) stillness, (2) clarity in vision, and (3) restoration of peace through active rest. You might be tempted to identify more, but three is enough to stay focused on for the duration of the cleanse. More than likely, you will gain clarity on other things during this time anyway. So stick to three, ok?

3. **Ground Your Cleanse**
    Pick a scripture/sura, a quote, or affirming phrase as a grounding reflection for the cleanse. Write your grounding reflection down and hang it as many places as you can so that you are surrounded by this message during the week.

4. **Daily Reflection and Meditation**
    You'll need to break your grounding reflection up so that you can focus on a small part of it for the seven days. You might only select one word or a section of words of the grounding reflection to focus on each day. This will really depend on how long your grounding reflection is.

5. **Identify 3 study resources**
    Books, workbooks, working journals, industry magazine, etc. that you can work through during this week. Use your time to study or read (audible books are good too).

6. **Get a new notebook**
    Just for this cleanse and write down thoughts, dreams, visions, ideas that come to you during this time.

CLARITY CLEANSE DAY 0-7 NOTES

Day Zero (anytime before 11:59pm on your Day 1)

First, spend some time writing out the thoughts that are consuming your mind (whatever is worrying you, decisions you have to make, people that are on your mind, the things you are overthinking, any questions you may have). If you are a person of faith and there is something in particular that you know requires God's attention over the next 7 days, write it down. This is the time for you to get all of your scattered thoughts out before you start the cleanse. Think about what you want to see, hear, and achieve through the cleanse. Finally, make sure that you have 3-7 accountability partners that are cleansing also or that will check on you daily during the cleanse.

Days 1-7

Stay focused on your grounding reflection and focus areas. Don't seek out information or answers haphazardly. Be open to what flows to you during this time. Answers may appear as dreams, visions, bright ideas, or verbal confirmations through people you are connected to. Use this time to be grateful, thoughtful, and deliberate about your clarity of mind.

- No social media.

- No links, no likes, no shares.

- Turn your app notifications off.

- If TV is a major distraction for you, limit your tv time also.

- No toxic people or unnecessary drama during this time - you may have to take a break from some people.

In addition to your grounding reflection, you will need to replace your scattered thoughts with positive and pointed reflections. You will need to spend 5-10 (minimum) minutes in meditation. You can meditate to music, ambient sounds, or silence. Before you meditate, still yourself and try to quiet your thoughts so that your meditation time can be beneficial.

Positive Vibes, Peace, and Liberty to you as you seek clarity!

WORKS CITED OR REFERENCED FOR WRITING PURPOSES:

Consistently Lit:

- Cube, I. (Producer) & Raboy, M. (Director). (2002). Friday After Next. United States: New Line Cinema.

- Hahn, D. (Producer) & Allers, R., Minkoff, R. (Directors). (1994). The Lion King. United States: Walt Disney Pictures.

Journey/Evolution:

- van der Kolk, B. (2014). The Body Keeps The Score: Brain, Mind, and Body in the Healing of Trauma, New York: Penguin Books.

Trauma:

- Huncho Dreams [Recorded by Quavo]. Quavo Huncho [Studio Album]. Los Angeles, CA: Capital Records.

Mindwholeness:

- Triggered [Recorded by Jhene Aiko]. Single [Digital Download]. New York City, NY: Def Jam Recordings.

- Lomas, T. (2016, March). Where Does the Word Mindfulness Come From? Retrieved from https://www.psychologytoday.com/us/blog/mindfulness-wellbeing/201603/where-does-the-word-mindfulness-come

- Bell, S., Sheckley, B. (2006). Experience, Consciousness, and Learning: Implications for Instruction. New Directions for Adult and Continuing Education (43-53). San Francisco: Jossey Bass.

- Wolfe, P. (2006). The Role of Meaning and Emotion in Learning. New Directions for Adult and Continuing Education (35-41). San Francisco: Jossey Bass.

WORKS CITED OR REFERENCED FOR WRITING PURPOSES:

Own Your Shit

- Walker, M. (2017). Quotes retrieved from various videos retrieved from https://www.youtube.com/channel/UCXqcrtyJryKeb37iDrLphmw

Grace

- Lucado, M. (2014). Grace: More Than We Deserve, Greater Than We Imagine. City, State: Thomas Nelson Publishers.

- Siu, B. (2018, April). Hit-and-Run Deaths at All-Time High, New AAA Study Says. Retrieved from https://abcnews. go.com › hit-run-deaths-time-high-aaa-study › story

Know Your Worth

- Huncho Dreams [Recorded by Quavo]. Quavo Huncho [Studio Album]. Los Angeles, CA: Capital Records.

- Top Off [Recorded by DJ Khaled, Jay-Z, Future, and B]. Father of Ashad [Studio Album]. Los Angeles, CA: Epic Records.

- 0 to 100/The Catch Up [Recorded by Drake]. Single [Studio Recording]. New Orleans, LA: Young Money

- Everybody Mad [Recorded by O.T. Genasis]. Single [Digital Download]. Brooklyn, NY: Conglomerate.

- Mood4EVA [Recorded by Beyonce, Jay-Z, Childish Gambino, Oumou Sangare]. The Lion King: The Gift [Studio Album]. New York City, New York: Parkwood.

- Back On [Recorded by Lil' Baby]. Quality Control: Control The Streets, Vol. 2 [Studio Album]. Atlanta, GA: Quality Control.

Meet the Author

Ayana Thomas has demonstrated success in people development as an organizational consultant and counselor in federal government, higher education, private sector, and religious organizations. Her goal is to help people reach and then succeed at their highest potential. Whether it's influencing people in a 1-1 setting or teaching a group, Ayana believes that we are all purposed to do great things. Ayana founded Liberty Writes, LLC. and wrote Life Light, to help people all over the world pursue powered living.

For upcoming appearances and books, visit ayanathomas.com.

Liberty
Writes

LIBERTY WRITES IS HERE TO HELP YOU!

Liberty Writes is a people development brand that focuses on building the whole person. The brand offers career, family, and organizational development services.

Visit ayanathomas.com to learn more!

www.ingramcontent.com/pod-product-compliance
Lightning Source LLC
Chambersburg PA
CBHW072143020426
42334CB00018B/1862